Billie Holiday Anthology

"Lady Day" Had A Right To Sing The Blues by Leonard Feather
Complete Sheet Music Editions

D1602073

005046 285786 00504

A Publication of
CREATIVE CONCEPTS PUBLISHING CORP.
Catalog # 07-1019
ISBN # 1-56922-008-5

Produced by John L. Haag

Exclusive Distributor:
CREATIVE CONCEPTS PUBLISHING CORPORATION
6020-B Nicolle Street, Ventura, California 93003
Check out our Web site at *http://www.creativeconcepts.com*
or you can Email us at *mail@creativeconcepts.com*

CONTENTS

LADY DAY HAD A RIGHT TO SING THE BLUES

By LEONARD FEATHER

Eleanora Fagan McKay, whom the world remembers best as Billie Holiday and whom Lester Young nicknamed "Lady Day," was born on April 7, 1915.

There will, of course, be no national commemoration of her birthday, nothing like the huge ceremony that was held on Duke Ellington's birthday when he was honored by the issuance of a U.S. Postage Stamp with his likeness.

Ellington, who came to fame early, never had to deal with traumas such as those endured by Holiday during her relatively brief years of prominence. In fact, given the conditions under which she grew up, and the sheer chance incidents that led to her discovery, we are lucky to have known her at all. Her autobiography, "Lady Sings the Blues," written for her by William Dufty, is best remembered for its opening sentence: "Mom and Pop were just a couple of kids when they got married; he was 18, she was 16 and I was three."

Pop was Clarence Holiday, a guitarist who played in the bands of Fletcher Henderson, Benny Carter and Don Redman. The Holiday marriage was short-lived. Raised by her mother, Billie (who took the name from her favorite silent-movie star, Billie Dove) got as far as the fifth grade in school, picked up nickels scrubbing the doorsteps of white families, and ran errands for prostitutes in a whorehouse. "I'm not the only one who heard their first good jazz in a whorehouse," she said in her book. "But...if I'd heard Louis Armstrong and Bessie Smith at a Girl Scout jamboree, I'd have loved it just the same."

According to her version, Billie was never a prostitute herself in Baltimore, but was raped in the house when she was 10, was arrested and sentenced to do penance in a Catholic institution.

After her release, whe went with her mother to New York. "Mom got me a room in a beautiful apartment belonging to a lady named Florence Williams." What Mom failed to observe was that Florence was one of the biggest madams in Harlem. Billie said that within days she had her chance to become a strictly $20 call girl - "and I took it."

Arrested again, she was sent to Welfare Island for four months, then wandered through Harlem looking for a job. At one club, Pod's and Jerry's, she auditioned as a dancer, failed, and was asked whether she could sing. She sang "Travelin' All Alone," was hired, and soon found herself earning a salary.

In 1933, at the Log Cabin, celebrities began to patronize the room: Paul Muni, John Hammond, Red Norvo, Mildred Bailey. Hammond brought Benny Goodman, who hired her to sing on two numbers on a record date. After the Log Cabin came the Hotcha and Dickie Wells' club and even the Apollo, for a munificent $50 a week.

John Hammond eventually found her regular recording work as the vocalist with Teddy Wilson and his various recording groups. A year after that series, she also began recording regularly under her own imprimatur. I was at the first "Billie Holiday and Her Orchestra" session, as Hammond's guest. Artie Shaw and Bunny Berigan were sidemen on the date. Billie sang two pop tunes of the day and poured her soul into "Summertime" (then a new song, too, since "Porgy and Bess" only had recently closed on Broadway).

When Billie had trouble with the fourth song, John Hammond called out from the control booth, "Billie, why don't you just sing some blues?"

"Billie's Blues," the product of that suggestion, was the first of a handful of songs in that idiom recorded by her. Though branded in the media (and by her book title) as a blues singer, she sang pop tunes and superior standard favorites almost exclusively; in fact, her only other celebrated blues was "Fine and Melow," immortalized in her TV appearance on "The Sound of Jazz."

I suppose that when I spent an evening at her home (shortly after her stint with the Count Basie band), it was the first time she had ever been interviewed. Her mother, an enormous but very short woman with a kindly manner, was as unaware as I of Billie's private indulgences; the heavy drinking and pot smoking were part of a life she lived away from home.

When she joined Artie Shaw, the first black singer with a white band, this was a unique event; I took a train to Boston for her opening night. There they sat, at opposite ends of the bandstand, Billie and Helen Forrest, the white "protection" vocalist who sang on most of the band's records (Billie was under contract to another company). Shaw was very protective, but the insults were too much, and Billie finally quit in disgust on being told to use the back door — ironically, when the band was playing in a hotel named after Abraham Lincoln.

The golden years for Lady Day began with her long tenure at Cafe Society, the Greenwich Village club where both the show and the audience were integrated, a rarity then. She sang her own "God Bless the Child." In 1939, she introduced "Strange Fruit," the song about a lynching. Soon she was working at the 52nd Street clubs, where she could elicit pin-drop silence from a crowd of noisy drinkers.

The producer Milt Bagler signed her for Decca records and asked her to record a new song, "Lover Man." "I want to do it with strings," Billie insisted. She got her way, and this became one of a long line of songs indelibly associated with her. One was her own "Don't Explain," inspired by an incident involving her husband, Jimmie Munroe. It was after her marriage to Monroe, she wrote, that the involvement with hard drugs began: first opium, then heroin. While wining an Esquire award every year, singing at the Metropolitan Opera House and the Los Angeles Philharmonic (where Jerome Kern presented her with the "Esky" statuette), she was sinking deeper into a morass that inevitably led to her arrest.

One of my bittersweet memories is the farewell concert she gave at Carnegie Hall just before reporting to the federal authorities. She sang "I'll Be Seeing You," and if there were any dry eyes in the house, I failed to observe them.

Billie was released from the Alderson, W.Va., women's facility looking healthy, even overweight. One night, she came over to cook dinner for my wife and me. On hearing that we were about to become parents, she said, "Wonderful! I want to be the godmother." When Billie Lorraine Feather was born, her godmother knitted her a pair of booties.

It had long amazed me that Billie had never played outside the United States. I assembled a show called "Jazz Club U.S.A." with her as the star, and the Red Norvo Trio, the Buddy De Franco Quartet and the all-female trio of the pianist Beryl Booker.

We opened in Stockholm in January, 1954, after the first of a series of disasters: Bad weather bumped our plane in Copenhagen and we straggled in by train a few hours before the first show.

In place of the ghetto theaters and sleazy dressing rooms that had marked too much of her life at home, Billie soon found herself besieged by autograph hunters, by fans bringing her bouquets on stage and treating her in a manner so deferential that she reacted accordingly. Her morale was never better.

Back home after that encouraging tour, she soon was surrounded by the old gang of hangers-on and pushers. By now she was recording for Norman Granz on Verve, but the strain of her life style had caught up with her vocal control; her final five years produced some sides worthy of her, along with several that revealed the toll taken on her range and her intonation. There was another arrest in 1956. Louis McKay, whom she had married around this time, moved to California.

In the fall of 1958, Billie agreed to make guest appearances at two concerts I had organized with a history of jazz format. A few old friends were there: Buck Clayton from the old Basie orchestra and George Auld of the Shaw band. Backstage, she told my wife: "I'm so goddamn lonely — since Louis and I broke up I got nobody, nothing."

We lived not far apart on the Upper West Side. After hearing about the death of Lester Young, to whom she had been so close in the Basie days, I dropped by to pick her up and take her to the funeral. In the taxi on the way downtown, she was sunk in gloom. "I'll be the next one to go," she said.

She was. Two months later, there was a pitiful final appearance in a benefit at the Phoenix Theatre for which Steve Allen and I were emcees. She looked so emaciated that I called Joe Glaser, her manager; the next morning we met at her apartment. He begged her to put herself in the hospital. "No, I'll be all right; the doctor said these shots he's giving me will do it. I've got to open in Montreal next Monday."

That was seven days away. On the following Saturday, she collapsed and was carried first to one hospital, then another. In a gruesome finale, she was arrested on her death bed for possession; police were posted outside her room. On admission to the hospital, she had some money strapped to her leg and almost nothing in her back account.

She died on July 17, 1959.

On April 7, 1986, near the corner of Vine Street and Selma Avenue in Hollywood, a star carrying her name was implanted in the sidewalk. Almost 27 years after she died in a New York hospital bed at the age of 44, Holiday at last made Tinseltown's Walk of Fame.

Her records are still with us, and the better-late-than-never Hollywood sidewalk star may remind a few stragglers that she was, as every singer from Frank Sinatra to some of today's ingenues have agreed, the ultimate jazz singer.

As I once wrote in a retrospective essay, her voice was the voice of living intensity, of soul in the true sense of that greatly abused word. As a human being, she was sweet, sour, kind, mean, generous, profane, lovable and impossible, and nobody who knew her expects to see anyone quite like her ever again.

Reprinted by Permission of Leonard Feather.

Billie Holiday (pictured with Jimmy Davis, co-composer of Lover Man).

AIN'T MISBEHAVIN'

Words by Andy Razaf
Music by Thomas "Fats" Waller and Harry Brooks

ALL OF ME

**Words and Music by
Seymour Simons and Gerald Marks**

out you.___ Take my lips___ I want to lose them,___ Take my arms___ I'll nev-er use them, Your good-bye___ left me with eyes that cry,___ How can I___

BABY, GET LOST

Words and Music by Leonard Feather

DO NOTHIN' TILL YOU HEAR FROM ME

Lyric by Bob Russell
Music by Duke Ellington

Verse:

| G | Gmaj 7 | G7 | E7 | Am | D9 | G |

Some - one told some - one and some - one told you but they would-n't hurt

| G#dim | D9 | G | G7 | E7 | A7 | D9 |

you not much, Since ev - 'ry - one spreads the sto - ry with his own lit - tle per - son - al touch.

Chorus:

| G | Gmaj7 | G7 | Cmaj7 |

Do noth- in' till you hear from me. Pay no at -ten-tion to what's said

DO IT AGAIN!

Words by B.G. DeSylva
Music by George Gershwin

CALL IT STORMY MONDAY

Words and Music by Aaron "T-Bone" Walker

EXTRA LYRICS

2

Yes, the eagle flies on Friday,
And Saturday I go out to play __
Eagle flies on Friday,
And Saturday I go out to play..
Sunday I go to church,
Then I kneel down to pray.

3

Lord have mercy,
Lord have mercy on me __
Lord have mercy,
My heart's in misery.
Crazy 'bout my baby,
Yes, send her back to me.

CRAZY HE CALLS ME

Words by Bob Russell
Music by Carl Sigman

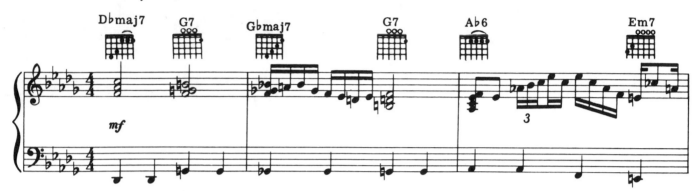

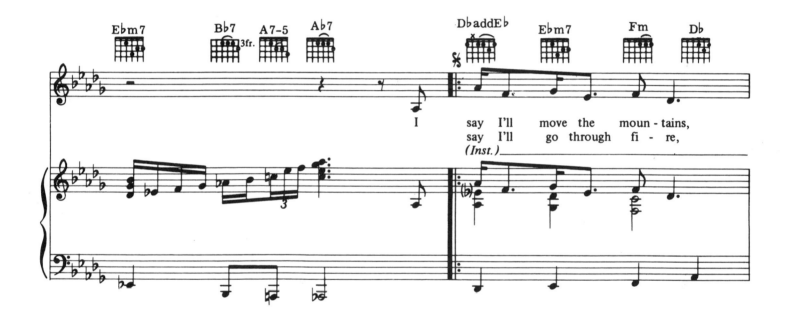

I say I'll move the moun-tains,
say I'll go through fi - re,
(Inst.)_____

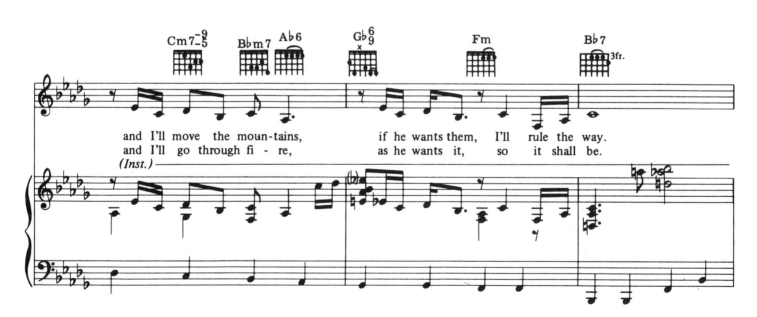

and I'll move the moun-tains,   if he wants them,   I'll rule the way.
and I'll go through fi - re,   as he wants it,   so it shall be.
(Inst.)_____

'TAIN'T NOBODY'S BIZ-NESS, IF I DO

Words and Music by Porter Grainger and Everett Robbins

VERSE

1. There ain't noth-in' I can do, nor noth-in' I can say,
2. Aft-er all, the way to do is do just as you please,

That folks don't crit-i-cize me;
Re-gard-less of their talk-in';

But I'm gon-na do just as I want to an-y-way,
Of-ten times the ones that talk will get down on their knees,

37

DO YOU KNOW WHAT IT MEANS TO MISS NEW ORLEANS?

Lyric by Eddie DeLange
Music by Louis Alter

I nev-er had this kind-a feel-in',_____

With drag-gin' heart and brain a-reel-in'._____ What's the mat-ter here's the mat-ter,_ Here's the thing that's real-ly wrong with me:

FIND OUT WHAT THEY LIKE AND HOW THEY LIKE IT

Words by Andy Razaf
Music by Thomas "Fats" Waller and Harry Brooks

BABY, WON'T YOU PLEASE COME HOME?

Words and Music by Charles Warfield and Clarence Williams

I CAN'T GIVE YOU ANYTHING BUT LOVE

Words by Dorothy Fields
Music by Jimmy McHugh

I Can't Give You An - y - thing But Love, Ba - by, ___

That's the on - ly thing I've plen - ty of,

FOR ALL WE KNOW

Lyric by Sam M. Lewis
Music by J. Fred Coots

NOBODY KNOWS YOU WHEN YOU'RE DOWN & OUT

Words and Music by Jimmie Cox

might-y fine time,___ Drink-ing high-price liq-uor, cham-pagne, and wine.___

When I be-gan___ to fall so low,___ I did-n't have a friend and

no place to go. If I ev-er get my hands on a

dol-lar a-gain,___ I'm gon-na hold on to it till the ea-gle grins.___

might-y strange,_____ with-out a doubt _____

No - bo-dy knows you when you're
No gal can use you when you're

down and out._____ down _____ and __ out, I mean:__

When __ you're down __ and _ out. _____

GUILTY

Words and Music by Gus Kahn,
Harry Akst and Richard A. Whiting

I CRIED FOR YOU

Words and Music by Arthur Freed, Gus Arnheim and Abe Lyman

All you did was laugh at me but things are dif-f'rent now.
But the slave that was all yours and now at last is free.

I CRIED _____ FOR YOU _____ Now it's

your turn to cry o - ver me._____

Ev - 'ry road has a turn - ing

I GOT IT BAD (And That Ain't Good)

Words and Music by Duke Ellington and Paul Francis Webster

The po-ets say that all who love are blind; But

I'm in love and I___ know what time it is!___ The

Good Book says "Go seek and ye shall find." Well,

DON'T TAKE YOUR LOVE FROM ME

Words and Music by Henry Nemo

I'LL BE AROUND

Words and Music by Alec Wilder

I'LL GET BY (As Long As I Have You)

Words by Roy Turk
Music by Fred E. Ahlert

I'M A FOOL TO WANT YOU

Words and Music by Jack Wolf, Joel Herron and Frank Sinatra

THE BIRTH OF THE BLUES

Words by B.G. DeSylva and Lew Brown
Music by Ray Henderson

IT HAD TO BE YOU

Words by Gus Kahn
Music by Isham Jones

I'VE GOT THE WORLD ON A STRING

Words by Ted Koehler
Music by Harold Arlen

(I'm Afraid)
THE MASQUERADE IS OVER

Words by Herb Magidson
Music by Allie Wrubel

Moderately slow
Eb Ebmaj7 Gm7-5 C7-9 Fm Bb7-9 Ebmaj7
My blue ho - ri - zon is turn - ing gray — And my dreams are
Eb7 Abm6 Bb7 CHORUS Eb G7
drift - ing a - way.
Your eyes don't shine — like they
words don't mean — what they
Cm Cm7 Bbm7 Eb9 Eb7 Ab C7 F7
used to shine And the thrill is gone — when your lips meet
used to mean. They were once in - spired, — now they're just rou -

THE JOINT IS JUMPIN'

Words by Andy Razaf and J.C. Johnson
Music by Thomas "Fats" Waller

Tempo di-sturb de neighbors

They have a new ex-pres-sion a-long old Har-lem way___ that tells you when a par-ty is ten times more___ than gay.___ To say that things are jump-in' leaves not a sin-gle doubt___ that

98

MAYBE YOU'LL BE THERE

Words by Sammy Gallop
Music by Rube Bloom

NO MORE

Lyric by Bob Russell
Music by Tutti Camarata

Nev - er felt so good be - fore _____ You're

down to my size, it's o-ver and done, So High-ness step down from your throne, That

look in your eyes don't both-er me, none can take you or leave you a-

lone. From my win-dow skies ain't gray No More, not

now. Here's the day that I've been wait-ing for,_____ Got

on-ly one heart, one heart with no spares must save it for lov-in', Some-

bod-y who cares, So you ain't gon-na both-er me No More

No MORE._____ MORE._____

MEAN TO ME

Words and Music by Fred E. Ahlert and Roy Turk

MIDNIGHT SUN

Words and Music by Johnny Mercer, Sonny Burke and Lionel Hampton

WE'LL BE TOGETHER AGAIN

Lyrics by Frankie Lane
Music by Carl Fischer

THERE'LL BE SOME CHANGES MADE

Words by Billy Higgins
Music by W. Benton Overstreet

I'M THE LONESOMEST GAL IN TOWN

Words by Lew Brown
Music by Albert Von Tilzer

ST. LOUIS BLUES (Pop Song Version)

Words and Music by W.C. Handy
New Arrangement by Leonard Moss

man's got a heart like a rock cast in the sea

or else he would-n't' have gone so far from me.

Well I love that man like a

school-boy loves his pie,

Like an

old Ken -tuck -y Col' -nel loves his rocks loves his rocks and rye, And I

love my ba - by till the day I die. __ Got the

Saint Lou -is Blues __ *(in the morn -ing)* Saint Lou -is Blues __ *(in the eve -ning)*

ADDITIONAL CHORUS LYRICS

A black headed woman makes a freight train jump the track,
Said a black headed woman makes a freight train jump the track.
But a long tall gal makes a preacher Ball the Jack.

Lord, a blonde headed woman makes a good man leave town,
Said a blonde headed woman makes a good man leave town.
But a red head woman makes a boy slap his papa down.

Oh, ashes to ashes and dust to dust,
I said ashes to ashes and dust to dust.
If my blues don't get you, my jazzing must.

STORMY WEATHER
(Keeps Rainin' All The Time)

Lyric by Ted Koehler
Music by Harold Arlen

Slow Lament

TEACH ME TONIGHT

Words by Sammy Cahn
Music by Gene De Paul

131

THAT OLE DEVIL CALLED LOVE

Words and Music by Doris Fisher and Allan Roberts

Medium Slow Blues Tempo

VERSE

Some-one's whis-p'rin' in my ear I say no no go a-way but he don't hear,— He fol-lows me a-round,— builds me up— tears me down,—I try my best to shake him but he just hangs a-round.

Ad Lib Tempo Follow Voice

CHORUS

UNTIL THE REAL THING COMES ALONG

Words and Music by Mann Holiner, Alberta Nichols, Sammy Cahn, Saul Chaplin and L. E. Freeman

words can't ex- plain my love and its worth.___
some- what con- veys the way that I feel.___

This much I know is true,
I met with no suc- cess;

There'll
I'm

nev- er be an- oth- er you. That's why
strict- ly on my own I guess. And so

REFRAIN
Slowly, with expression

I'd work for you, I'd slave for you,

poco rit.

p - mf

WHEN IT'S SLEEPY TIME DOWN SOUTH

Words and Music by Leon Rene, Otis Rene and Clarence Muse

WHAT'S NEW?

Words by Johnny Burke
Music by Bob Haggart

WHEN YOU'RE SMILING
(The Whole World Smiles With You)

Words and Music by Mark Fisher, Joe Goodwin and Larry Shay

Slowly, with expression

WHEN YOU'RE SMIL – ING,_____ WHEN YOU'RE

SMIL – ING,_____ the whole world smiles with

you,_____ When you're laugh - ing,_____ When you're

laugh - ing,_____ The sun comes shin - ing

YOU'RE MY THRILL

Words by Sidney Clare
Music by Jay Gorney

YOU BETTER GO NOW

Words by Bickley (Bix) Reichner
Music by Robert Graham

love, And the way I feel it must be spring. I want you

so now,—— You have the lips I love to touch; You bet-ter go now,——

You bet-ter go, be-cause I like you much too

1. much. 2. You bet-ter much.

TRAVELIN' LIGHT

Words by Sidney Clare
Music by Harry Akst